Chapter 1: Understanding the Raw Diet

To fully grasp the benefits of feeding dogs a raw diet, it is crucial to explore their evolutionary background. Before dogs became domesticated, their ancestors, wolves, thrived in the wild by consuming a diet predominantly composed of raw meat, bones, and organs. This natural diet played a vital role in their survival and overall health.

Beyond the wolf ancestors, researchers and experts have also studied the dietary habits of other canids and their potential influence on the modern dog's raw diet. One theory is based on the concept of "primordial dog diets," which suggests that before wolves, there were canids that were more scavengers than hunters, relying on the leftovers and scraps from human settlements. These early canids might have had access to a variety of foods, including raw meat, bones, plant matter, and even occasional cooked leftovers. This theory suggests that the modern dog's digestive system is well-adapted to handle a diverse range of foods, supporting the idea that a raw diet can be beneficial.

Feeding dogs a raw diet offers a myriad of benefits that contribute to their overall health and well-being. Let's delve into some of the key advantages:

Enhanced Digestion: Dogs possess relatively short and acidic digestive tracts, ideal for breaking down and assimilating raw meat. A raw diet promotes optimal digestion, reduces the risk of digestive disorders, and often results in smaller, firmer stools.

Healthy Skin and Coat: Raw diets provide dogs with essential fatty acids, including omega-3 and omega-6, which are vital for maintaining healthy skin and a lustrous coat. These nutrients can help alleviate itching, inflammation, and allergies, ensuring your dog's skin remains supple and their coat gleams.

Dental Health: Chewing on raw meaty bones serves as a natural toothbrush for dogs. This action helps clean their teeth, reduce plaque buildup, prevent tartar formation, and mitigate the risk of gum disease. Additionally, the gnawing motion strengthens their jaw muscles and provides mental stimulation.

Improved Energy and Vitality: A balanced raw diet supplies dogs with high-quality proteins, essential amino acids, vitamins, and minerals. This nutrient-dense diet fuels their energy levels, aids in muscle development, and contributes to their overall vitality.

While raw feeding has gained popularity, there are some misconceptions and concerns that need to be addressed. It's important to have accurate information to make informed decisions about your dog's diet. Let's address a few common misconceptions:

Bacterial Contamination: Raw diets can be wrongly associated with a higher risk of bacterial contamination, such as Salmonella or E. coli. However, with proper handling, sourcing quality ingredients, and implementing hygiene practices, the risk can be minimized significantly.

Nutritional Imbalance: Critics argue that raw diets may lack essential nutrients, leading to nutritional imbalances. However, when appropriately formulated and balanced, raw diets can provide all the necessary nutrients dogs need for optimal health.

Dental Hazards: Concerns about dental hazards, such as cracked teeth or choking, when feeding raw bones need to be addressed. Choosing appropriate bone sizes and closely supervising chewing sessions can mitigate these risks.

Understanding and addressing these misconceptions and concerns will enable you to make well-informed decisions and navigate the journey of feeding your dog a raw diet confidently. By delving into the evolutionary background of dogs, exploring the benefits of a raw diet, considering the concept of primordial dog diets, and debunking common misconceptions, this chapter aims to provide you with a solid foundation of knowledge.

Chapter 2: The Nutritional Requirements of Dogs

Dogs, like all living beings, have specific nutritional requirements to support their growth, development, and overall well-being. Understanding these requirements is crucial for providing a balanced and nutritious raw diet. Essential nutrients are the building blocks that dogs require for proper functioning and health. They include proteins, fats, carbohydrates, vitamins, minerals, and water.

Proteins: Proteins are vital for dogs as they provide amino acids necessary for growth, repair of tissues, and the production of enzymes and hormones. High-quality animal proteins, such as those found in raw meat, poultry, and fish, are crucial for meeting a dog's protein requirements.

Fats: Fats are a concentrated source of energy and provide essential fatty acids, such as omega-3 and omega-6, which play a crucial role in maintaining healthy skin and coat, supporting brain function, and promoting overall cellular health. Including fats from sources like raw meats, fish, and oils in the diet is important.

Carbohydrates: While dogs are primarily carnivores, they can still derive some benefits from carbohydrates. Carbohydrates provide energy and can be sourced from fruits, vegetables, and grains (if included in the diet). However, it's important to note that dogs have a limited ability to digest and utilize carbohydrates compared to other nutrients.

Vitamins: Vitamins are essential for various bodily functions, such as maintaining a healthy immune system, promoting growth, and supporting metabolism. A well-balanced raw diet that includes a variety of fruits and vegetables can provide dogs with the necessary vitamins, but certain vitamins (e.g., vitamin D) may require supplementation.

Minerals: Minerals, such as calcium, phosphorus, iron, and zinc, are vital for strong bones and teeth, nerve function, oxygen transport, and overall cellular health. Organ meats, bones, and a diverse range of fruits and vegetables can supply dogs with essential minerals.

Water: Water is a fundamental nutrient that is necessary for a dog's survival. Ensure that your dog always has access to clean and fresh water to prevent dehydration and support vital bodily functions.

Macronutrients: Proteins, Fats, and Carbohydrates:

Understanding the role of macronutrients in a dog's diet is crucial for providing a balanced raw diet.

Proteins: Dogs have a higher protein requirement compared to many other animals. Protein provides the necessary amino acids for muscle development, tissue repair, and the production of enzymes and hormones. When feeding a raw diet, it is important to include a variety of protein sources, such as lean meats, organ meats, and eggs, to ensure a complete amino acid profile.

Fats: Fats are a concentrated source of energy for dogs and are essential for various bodily functions. They provide omega-3 and omega-6 fatty acids, which support healthy skin and coat, reduce inflammation, and promote proper brain function. Including fatty cuts of meat, fish, and oils like salmon oil or flaxseed oil in the diet can help meet a dog's fat requirements.

Carbohydrates: While dogs have a limited need for carbohydrates, they can still benefit from small amounts. Carbohydrates provide energy and fiber. When including carbohydrates in a raw diet, opt for low-glycemic options like leafy greens, broccoli, and berries, which provide essential nutrients without causing spikes in blood sugar.

Micronutrients:

Micronutrients, including vitamins and minerals, are essential for a dog's overall health and well-being. They play a crucial role in various bodily functions, including immune support, bone health, enzyme reactions, and maintaining healthy organs.

Vitamins: Dogs require a range of vitamins, including vitamin A, vitamin D, vitamin E, vitamin K, and the B-complex vitamins (thiamin, riboflavin, niacin, etc.). These vitamins are involved in numerous metabolic processes, vision, immune function, and overall health. While a raw diet rich in a variety of fruits and vegetables can provide many vitamins, it is important to ensure that all necessary vitamins are adequately supplied.

Consult with a veterinarian or a canine nutritionist to determine if vitamin supplementation is necessary.

Minerals: Minerals, such as calcium, phosphorus, iron, zinc, and others, are crucial for various bodily functions, including bone and teeth health, nerve transmission, and enzyme reactions. A balanced raw diet should include a variety of ingredients that naturally provide these minerals. Raw meaty bones, such as chicken wings or beef ribs, are excellent sources of calcium and phosphorus, while organ meats, such as liver and kidney, provide essential minerals like iron and zinc.

Calculating Your Dog's Nutritional Needs:

Calculating your dog's nutritional needs is essential to ensure they receive the right amount of nutrients for their size, age, and activity level. Factors to consider when determining your dog's nutritional needs include:

Life Stage: Puppies, adult dogs, and senior dogs have different nutritional requirements. Puppies require more protein and calories for growth, while senior dogs may need lower fat and calorie levels.

Size and Breed: Different dog breeds and sizes have varying metabolic rates and energy requirements. Larger breeds may need more calories, while smaller breeds may require less.

Activity Level: Dogs with high activity levels, such as working or sporting dogs, may require more calories and protein to support their energy needs. Less active or sedentary dogs may need fewer calories to prevent weight gain.

Individual Factors: Each dog is unique, and factors such as metabolism, health conditions, and reproductive status (intact or neutered) can impact their nutritional needs. Consult with a veterinarian or a canine nutritionist to determine the specific nutritional requirements for your dog.

By understanding the essential nutrients, the role of macronutrients and micronutrients, and how to calculate your dog's nutritional needs, you can ensure that your dog's raw diet meets their requirements for optimal health and well-being. In the next chapter, we will explore selecting the right ingredients for a balanced raw meal.

Chapter 3: Selecting the Right Ingredients

Feeding your dog a raw diet requires careful consideration of the ingredients you include to ensure a well-balanced and nutritious meal. In this chapter, we will explore the importance of selecting high-quality meats and poultry, incorporating organ meats, incorporating fruits and vegetables, and enhancing the diet with supplements. When it comes to selecting meats and poultry for your dog's raw diet, quality is paramount. Here are some key points to consider:

Freshness: Choose fresh, high-quality meats and poultry from reputable sources. Look for products that are labeled as human-grade or fit for human consumption, as they undergo strict quality control measures.

Variety: Incorporating a variety of meats and poultry ensures that your dog receives a wide range of nutrients. Consider including lean meats like beef, chicken, turkey, and lamb. Additionally, less common proteins like venison, duck, or bison can provide a novel and nutritious addition to their diet.

Organs: Organ meats are highly nutritious and should be included in your dog's raw diet. They are rich in essential vitamins, minerals, and amino acids. Good choices for organ meats include liver, kidney, heart, and spleen. Aim to include a variety of organs to provide a diverse nutrient profile.

Bones: Raw meaty bones are an essential part of a raw diet as they provide necessary minerals, dental benefits, and mental stimulation. Choose bones that are appropriate for your dog's size and breed. For example, larger dogs can handle larger bones like beef knuckles or marrow bones, while smaller dogs may require smaller options such as chicken wings or necks.

While dogs are primarily carnivorous, incorporating a variety of fruits and vegetables can provide additional nutrients and fiber to their raw diet. Here are some considerations:

Nutrient-Rich Choices: Include fruits and vegetables that are safe and beneficial for dogs. Examples include leafy greens like spinach or kale, cruciferous vegetables like broccoli or cauliflower, and colorful options like blueberries or carrots. Avoid toxic foods like grapes, raisins, onions, or garlic.

Preparation: Fruits and vegetables should be washed thoroughly to remove any potential pesticides or contaminants. Some vegetables may require steaming or lightly cooking to improve digestibility for dogs.

Variety and Moderation: While fruits and vegetables can be valuable additions to a dog's diet, they should not make up most of their meals. Aim for a balanced ratio of about 80% meat and 20% fruits and vegetables. Each dog is unique, so adjust the ratio based on your dog's specific needs and preferences.

Supplements can play a role in ensuring your dog's nutritional needs are met. Here are some important considerations:

Omega-3 Fatty Acids: Supplementing with omega-3 fatty acids, such as fish oil or algae oil, can provide additional support for your dog's skin, coat, and overall health. These supplements help reduce inflammation and support brain function.

Probiotics: Probiotics can aid in maintaining a healthy gut microbiome. They promote digestion, strengthen the immune system, and help prevent digestive issues. Look for high-quality probiotic supplements specifically formulated for dogs.

Joint Supplements: Dogs, especially larger breeds or senior dogs, may benefit from joint supplements that support cartilage health and mobility. Glucosamine, chondroitin, and MSM are common ingredients found in joint supplements for dogs.

Individual Needs: Consult with a veterinarian or a canine nutritionist to determine if your dog requires any specific supplements based on their breed, age, health conditions, or individual needs. They can provide guidance on appropriate dosages and ensure that the supplements you choose are safe and effective for your dog.

It's important to remember that every dog is unique, and their nutritional requirements may vary based on factors such as age, breed, size, activity level, and overall health. As you prepare your dog's raw diet, pay attention to their individual needs and make adjustments accordingly.

Once you've transitioned your dog to a raw diet, closely monitor their health and well-being. Keep an eye on their weight, energy levels, coat condition, and overall vitality. Regular visits to the veterinarian are essential to ensure that your dog is thriving on their new diet. If your dog has been on a different diet, such as a commercial kibble, transitioning them to a raw diet should be done gradually. Sudden changes can cause digestive upset. Slowly introduce raw foods into their diet while reducing the amount of their current food over several days.

A balanced raw diet is just one aspect of your dog's overall health. Regular exercise and mental stimulation are equally important for their well-being. Ensure your dog gets enough physical activity and mental enrichment through playtime, training sessions, and interactive toys. While a raw diet can be beneficial for many dogs, some may have specific dietary issues or health conditions that require special consideration. If you notice any adverse reactions or health concerns, consult with your veterinarian or a qualified canine nutritionist to address these issues effectively.

Feeding your dog a raw diet can be a rewarding and beneficial experience. By understanding their evolutionary background, nutritional requirements, and the importance of high-quality ingredients, you can create a balanced and nutritious diet for your canine companion. Remember to tailor the diet to your dog's individual needs and monitor their health regularly.

While transitioning to a raw diet requires careful planning and consideration, the potential benefits, including improved digestion, healthier skin and coat, and enhanced vitality, can make it all worthwhile. Providing your dog with the best possible nutrition through a thoughtfully prepared raw diet is a meaningful way to show your love and care for your loyal and beloved companion. So, embark on this journey of canine wellness and enjoy the rewarding experience of nourishing your dog with a wholesome and balanced raw diet.

Chapter 4: Preparing a Balanced Raw Meal

Preparing a balanced raw meal for your dog is crucial for their optimal health. In this chapter, we will cover important aspects of proper food handling and storage, understanding the BARF (Biologically Appropriate Raw Food) model, balancing calcium and phosphorus, and creating variety for optimal nutrition.

Proper food handling and storage are vital to maintaining the freshness and safety of the raw ingredients used in your dog's meals. Here are some guidelines:

Hygiene: Wash your hands thoroughly before and after handling raw ingredients to prevent cross-contamination. Clean all utensils, cutting boards, and surfaces used for raw food preparation with hot, soapy water.

-**Storage**: Raw meat and poultry should be stored in a refrigerator or freezer to prevent spoilage and the growth of harmful bacteria. Use airtight containers or freezer bags to store raw ingredients separately from other foods to avoid contamination.

Thawing: When thawing frozen raw ingredients, do so in the refrigerator or use the defrost function in a microwave if immediate use is required. Avoid thawing at room temperature to prevent bacterial growth.

-**Safe** Handling: Handle raw ingredients with care to minimize the risk of foodborne illnesses. Clean any surfaces or utensils that meet raw meat or poultry to prevent the spread of bacteria.

The BARF model is a feeding approach that aims to provide dogs with a diet that closely resembles their natural, biologically appropriate diet. Here are some key principles:

-**Variety**: The BARF model emphasizes offering a variety of raw meats, poultry, organs, bones, fruits, and vegetables to ensure a diverse nutrient profile.

-**Raw** Meaty Bones: Raw meaty bones play a crucial role in the BARF model. They provide essential minerals, dental benefits, and mental stimulation. Choose appropriate bone sizes for your dog's safety and ensure they are suitable for the breed and size.

-**80-10-10 Ratio**: The BARF model suggests a general guideline of an 80-10-10 ratio for meat, bones, and organs. This ratio ensures a balanced diet, with 80% meat for protein and amino acids, 10% edible bone for calcium and phosphorus, and 10% organs (with half being liver) for essential vitamins and minerals.

-**Adjustments**: The BARF model allows for individual adjustments based on your dog's specific needs, such as activity level, age, and health conditions. Consult with a veterinarian or a canine nutritionist for personalized guidance.

Achieving the right balance of calcium and phosphorus is crucial for maintaining healthy bones and teeth in dogs. Consider the following:

-**Calcium Sources**: Raw meaty bones, such as chicken wings or beef ribs, are excellent sources of natural calcium. Choose bones that are appropriate for your dog's size and breed to ensure they can chew them safely and consume the bone.

-**Phosphorus Sources**: Meats and organs, such as beef, poultry, and liver, are reliable sources of phosphorus. Balancing the intake of calcium-rich bones with phosphorus-rich meats and organs helps maintain the proper calcium-to-phosphorus ratio.

-**Supplements**: In some cases, especially if feeding a homemade raw diet, it may be necessary to supplement with calcium or a calcium/phosphorus supplement to ensure the appropriate ratio is achieved. Consult with a veterinarian or a canine nutritionist for guidance on supplementation.

Providing a varied diet is key to ensuring your dog receives a wide range of nutrients. Consider the following guidelines:

-**Meat Selection**: Offer diverse types of meats such as beef, chicken, turkey, lamb, and fish. Each protein source provides a unique nutrient profile, ensuring a diverse array of essential amino acids and fatty acids.

-**Organ Variety**: Include a variety of organ meats in your dog's diet, such as liver, kidney, heart, and spleen. Each organ provides different essential nutrients, contributing to a well-rounded and balanced meal plan.

Fruits and Vegetables: Rotate a variety of fruits and vegetables in your dog's diet to provide different vitamins, minerals, and antioxidants. Experiment with options like broccoli, carrots, spinach, blueberries, and more.

Seasonal Ingredients: Incorporate seasonal ingredients to add variety and freshness to your dog's meals. Take advantage of locally available produce to provide nutrient-rich options during various times of the year.

Supplement Rotation: If using supplements, consider rotating them periodically to provide a variety of additional nutrients and prevent reliance on a single source.

In addition to preparing raw meals from scratch, there are commercial raw food options available that can provide convenience and ensure balanced nutrition. One such example is "Just Food For Dogs" (JFFD), a company that specializes in providing fresh, whole-food meals for dogs. Just Food For Dogs (JFFD) is a renowned company dedicated to offering human-grade, gently cooked, and fresh-frozen dog food made with high-quality ingredients. Their meals are formulated to meet the nutritional needs of dogs, including various life stages and specific dietary requirements.

JFFD uses only premium, human-grade ingredients to create their meals, which often include a variety of proteins like beef, chicken, turkey, fish, or lamb, combined with nutrient-rich fruits, vegetables, and essential supplements. The company prides itself on ensuring the quality and safety of their ingredients, providing dog owners with peace of mind. One of the benefits of incorporating JFFD into your dog's diet is the convenience it offers. The meals are pre-prepared and ready to serve, eliminating the need for extensive meal preparation. JFFD provides portioned meals that take the guesswork out of feeding, ensuring your dog receives the appropriate amount of food.

Another advantage of JFFD is their commitment to customization. They offer recipes tailored to dogs with specific dietary needs, such as allergies, sensitivities, weight management, or senior dogs. This level of customization allows you to address your dog's individual requirements and preferences effectively.

When transitioning your dog to JFFD, it is important to follow their specific transition guidelines. Gradually introduce the new food while reducing the previous diet to prevent digestive upset and allow your dog's system to adjust. Monitoring your dog's health and well-being during the transition period is essential, and you may need to adjust the portion sizes or ingredients as recommended by JFFD or your veterinarian.

Combining JFFD meals with homemade raw meals is also an option that offers a balance of convenience and customization. This allows you to incorporate the benefits of commercial raw food while still having the flexibility to add your own ingredients or recipes.

By considering Just Food For Dogs (JFFD) as a commercial raw food option, you can provide your dog with a balanced and convenient raw diet. Whether you choose to solely rely on JFFD meals or combine them with homemade recipes, follow the guidelines provided by the company and monitor your dog's health to ensure their nutritional needs are met.

Chapter 5: Transitioning to a Raw Diet

Transitioning your dog to a raw diet requires careful planning and a gradual adjustment to ensure a smooth transition. In this chapter, we will discuss the importance of transitioning, recommended transition timeline, monitoring your dog's health during the process, and troubleshooting common challenges that may arise.

Transitioning your dog to a raw diet is essential to allow their digestive system to adapt to the new food. Abruptly changing your dog's diet can lead to digestive upset, including diarrhea or vomiting. By gradually introducing the raw diet, you give their body time to adjust and minimize the risk of gastrointestinal issues. The transition timeline may vary depending on your dog's individual needs and sensitivity to dietary changes. Here is a general guideline to help you transition your dog to a raw diet:

Week 1: Start by substituting a small portion of your dog's current diet with a small portion of the new raw diet. Aim for a ratio of 75% old diet and 25% raw diet for the first few days.

Week 2: Gradually increase the proportion of the raw diet to 50%, while reducing the old diet to 50%. This allows your dog's digestive system to adapt to the new food gradually.

Week 3: Continue increasing the raw diet to 75% while reducing the old diet to 25%. Monitor your dog for any signs of digestive issues or allergies during this period.

Week 4: By the fourth week, your dog should be fully transitioned to the raw diet. They can now be fed 100% of the raw diet, and the previous diet can be completely eliminated.

Remember that this timeline is a general guideline, and you should adjust it based on your dog's individual response and tolerance to dietary changes. Some dogs may require a longer transition period, especially if they have sensitive stomachs or pre-existing digestive issues. During the transition period, it is crucial to closely monitor your dog's health and well-being. Keep an eye out for any signs of digestive upset, including loose stools, vomiting, or a decrease in appetite. Additionally, observe changes in your dog's energy levels, coat condition, and overall demeanor.

If you notice any concerning symptoms or if your dog is experiencing prolonged digestive issues, consult with a veterinarian. They can provide guidance and evaluate your dog's specific needs, ensuring a successful transition to a raw diet. Transitioning to a raw diet may present some challenges along the way. Here are a few common issues that may arise and some troubleshooting tips:

Digestive Upset: If your dog experiences loose stools or digestive upset during the transition, slow down the transition process. Go back to the previous stage where they had no digestive issues and maintain that ratio for a few more days before progressing.

Refusal to Eat: Some dogs may be hesitant to try new foods. If your dog refuses to eat the raw diet, try warming the food slightly or adding a small amount of bone broth or a natural topper to entice them. Gradually reduce the additions as your dog becomes more comfortable with the new diet.

Nutritional Imbalance: Ensuring a balanced diet is crucial. If you are preparing homemade meals, work with a veterinarian or a canine nutritionist to ensure the recipes meet your dog's nutritional needs. If feeding a commercial raw diet, choose a reputable brand that provides complete and balanced meals.

Transitioning from Kibble: Moving from a kibble-based diet to a raw diet can be a notable change for your dog. To ease the transition, consider gradually reducing the amount of kibble while increasing the raw diet portion.

Remember that every dog is unique, and the transition process may vary. Patience, close monitoring, and adjustments based on your dog's individual needs are key to a successful transition to a raw diet. Transitioning your dog to a raw diet can sometimes put strain on their digestive system as it adapts to the new food. To support your dog's digestive health during the transition, you may consider using digestive aids like FidoBiotics Good Guts or equivalent products.

Digestive aids are supplements designed to support and maintain a healthy digestive system in dogs. They often contain a blend of probiotics, prebiotics, enzymes, and other beneficial ingredients that help promote digestion, balance gut flora, and alleviate digestive upset. FidoBiotics Good Guts is one example of a digestive aid specifically formulated for dogs. It contains a blend of beneficial bacteria strains, including probiotics, along with prebiotic fibers to nourish the gut flora. This combination helps support digestion, nutrient absorption, and overall gut health.

Digestive aids can assist in the transition to a raw diet by promoting a healthy gut environment and reducing the risk of digestive issues such as diarrhea, gas, or bloating. They can also help ease the adjustment period, particularly for dogs with sensitive stomachs or those prone to digestive upset. Follow the specific instructions provided by the manufacturer for the proper dosage and administration of the digestive aid. It is often recommended to start using the supplement a few days before the transition to a raw diet and continue for a few weeks into the transition period. Monitor your dog's response and consult with a veterinarian if needed.

Digestive aids can complement the transition process, but they should not replace a balanced diet or veterinary advice. Ensure that your dog's raw diet is nutritionally complete and consult with a veterinarian or a canine nutritionist to address any specific concerns or dietary requirements. Remember that while digestive aids like FidoBiotics Good Guts can be helpful during the transition, every dog is unique, and individual responses may vary. Monitor your dog's digestive health and adjust the use of digestive aids as needed.

Chapter 6: Meal Preparation and Food Safety

Proper meal preparation and food safety are paramount when feeding your dog a raw diet. In this chapter, we will delve into the practical aspects of meal preparation, including sourcing ingredients, handling raw food, portioning meals, serving guidelines, and the crucial importance of preventing cross-contamination. When preparing raw meals for your dog, it is important to prioritize high-quality ingredients. Consider the following guidelines when sourcing ingredients:

Meat and Poultry: Choose fresh, human-grade meats and poultry from reputable sources. Look for products that are specifically labeled for human consumption to ensure quality and safety. Select lean cuts of meat to maintain a proper balance of fats and proteins.

Organ Meats: Opt for fresh organ meats such as liver, kidney, heart, and spleen. Ensure they are from trusted sources and handled with proper hygiene practices.

Fruits and Vegetables: Select fresh, organic options when possible. Wash fruits and vegetables thoroughly to remove any pesticides or contaminants. Avoid using toxic foods like grapes, raisins, onions, or garlic.

Supplements: Choose high-quality supplements from reputable brands. If necessary, consult with a veterinarian or a canine nutritionist for guidance on selecting appropriate supplements for your dog's specific needs.

Proper handling of raw food is essential to prevent the spread of bacteria and ensure food safety. Follow these guidelines when handling raw food for your dog:

Hygiene: Wash your hands thoroughly with soap and water before and after handling raw food. Clean all utensils, cutting boards, and surfaces that encounter raw meat or poultry to prevent cross-contamination.

Separation: Keep raw food separate from other foods, especially those that are consumed raw or require minimal cooking. Use separate cutting boards and utensils for raw food to avoid cross-contamination.

Cleaning: Regularly clean and sanitize food preparation surfaces, utensils, and storage containers to prevent the growth of harmful bacteria.

Thawing: Thaw raw meat and poultry in the refrigerator or using the defrost function in a microwave if immediate use is required. Avoid thawing at room temperature to minimize bacterial growth.

Proper portioning ensures that your dog receives an appropriate amount of food for their size and needs. Consider the following guidelines when portioning meals:

Dog's Weight and Activity Level: Consider your dog's weight, age, and activity level when determining the portion size. Guidelines provided by the food manufacturer, or a veterinarian can help you determine the appropriate amount to feed.

Percentage Method: Many raw feeding proponents recommend feeding dogs a percentage of their body weight. Common guidelines include feeding 2-3% of the dog's body weight for adult dogs and adjusting accordingly based on their activity level and weight management goals.

Meal Frequency: Depending on your dog's age and preference, divide the daily portion into one or two meals. Puppies and younger dogs typically require more frequent meals compared to adult dogs.

When serving raw meals to your dog, consider the following guidelines:

Temperature: Serve raw food at room temperature or slightly warmed to enhance palatability. Avoid serving food that is too hot or too cold.

Supervision: Always supervise your dog during mealtimes to ensure they chew bones thoroughly and eat safely. This is particularly important when feeding raw meaty bones.

Mealtime Duration: If your dog doesn't finish their meal within 15-20 minutes, remove the remaining food to prevent spoilage or bacterial growth. Avoid free feeding to maintain portion control and prevent overeating.

Preventing cross-contamination is crucial to ensure food safety for both your dog and your family. Pay close attention to the following:

Cleanliness: Maintain cleanliness in the kitchen by regularly cleaning surfaces, utensils, and equipment used for raw food preparation. Use hot, soapy water or disinfectants to sanitize effectively.

Separate Storage: Store raw food separately from other foods in airtight containers or freezer bags to prevent cross-contamination. Keep raw food stored in the lower portions of the refrigerator to prevent drips onto other foods.

Handling Utensils: Use separate cutting boards, knives, and utensils for raw food preparation. If possible, designate specific items solely for raw food use to avoid mixing with items used for cooked food.

Washing: Wash all utensils, cutting boards, and bowls used for raw food with hot, soapy water after each use. Consider using a dishwasher with a high-temperature sanitizing cycle if available.

By following proper meal preparation practices, ensuring food safety, and preventing cross-contamination, you can protect the health of both your dog and your family.

Chapter 7: Common Concerns and FAQs about Feeding a Raw Diet

Feeding a raw diet to your dog may raise various questions and concerns. In this chapter, we will address some of the most common concerns and provide answers to frequently asked questions to help you navigate the world of raw feeding with confidence. We will cover topics such as dental health, nutritional balance, food allergies, transitioning older dogs, and raw feeding on a budget.

One of the touted benefits of raw feeding is its positive impact on dental health. Here are some key points to consider:

Chewing Benefits: Raw meaty bones, a staple of raw diets, provide dogs with an opportunity to chew, promoting healthy teeth and gums. The gnawing action helps remove plaque and tartar buildup, reducing the risk of dental issues.

Supervised Chewing: It is important to supervise your dog during bone chewing to prevent any choking hazards or injuries. Choose appropriate bone sizes based on your dog's size and breed, and ensure they are able to handle them safely.

Dental Hygiene: While raw feeding can support dental health, it is still essential to practice good dental hygiene. Regular brushing of your dog's teeth, professional cleanings, and the use of dental chews or dental hygiene products recommended by your veterinarian are valuable additions to maintaining oral health.

Ensuring a nutritionally balanced diet is crucial for your dog's overall health. Here are some considerations:

Variety of Ingredients: Incorporating a variety of proteins, organ meats, fruits, and vegetables into your dog's raw diet helps provide a broad spectrum of essential nutrients.

Proportions: Aim for a general guideline of 80% meat, 10% edible bones, and 10% organs (with half being liver) in your dog's raw meals. This ratio helps provide a balanced intake of proteins, fats, vitamins, and minerals.

Individual Needs: Each dog has unique nutritional requirements based on factors such as age, breed, size, and activity level. Consult with a veterinarian or a canine nutritionist to tailor the diet to your dog's specific needs.

Raw feeding can be beneficial for dogs with food allergies or sensitivities. Here are a few points to consider:

Novel Proteins: Raw diets allow you to select proteins that your dog hasn't been exposed to before, which can be beneficial for dogs with allergies. Introduce new proteins gradually and monitor your dog for any adverse reactions.

Elimination Diets: Raw diets can be used as part of an elimination diet to identify specific allergens. By feeding a limited ingredient raw diet, you can isolate potential problem ingredients and reintroduce them systematically to determine any adverse reactions.

Consultation: If your dog has known food allergies or sensitivities, consult with a veterinarian or a canine nutritionist to create a customized raw diet that addresses their specific needs.

Transitioning older dogs to a raw diet may require additional considerations. Here's what you should keep in mind:

Gradual Transition: Older dogs may have more sensitive digestive systems, so a slow and gradual transition is especially important. Extend the transition timeline and monitor your dog closely for any signs of digestive upset.

Dental Health: Raw diets can benefit older dogs by promoting dental health, which is particularly important as dental issues become more common with age. Consult with your veterinarian for advice on appropriate bone choices for your senior dog.

Nutritional Requirements: Older dogs may have specific nutritional needs or health conditions that require modification of the raw diet. Work with a veterinarian or a canine nutritionist to ensure your senior dog's diet is appropriately balanced and tailored to their individual needs.

Feeding a raw diet doesn't have to break the bank. Here are some cost-saving tips:

Bulk Purchases: Buying ingredients in bulk, especially during sales or promotions, can help reduce costs. Consider connecting with local farmers or butchers who may offer discounted rates for raw feeding enthusiasts.

Seasonal and Local Produce: Incorporating seasonal and locally available fruits and vegetables can be more cost-effective. Visit farmers' markets or consider growing your own produce to save money.

DIY Preparation: Preparing meals at home allows you to control costs and adjust the diet based on your budget. However, ensure that the diet remains balanced and meets your dog's nutritional needs.

Commercial Raw Food: Commercial raw food options, like Just Food For Dogs, often offer a variety of meal plans at different price points. Evaluate the cost per meal and assess whether the convenience and nutritional balance provided by commercial options align with your budget.

Remember, maintaining the overall health and well-being of your dog should always be the priority, regardless of budget constraints. Consult with a veterinarian or a canine nutritionist to find the best balance between cost and nutritional quality for your dog's raw diet.

Chapter 8: Hygiene Practices and Bacterial Risks in Raw Feeding

Ensuring proper hygiene practices and understanding the potential bacterial risks associated with raw feeding is crucial for the safety of your dog and household. In this chapter, we will delve into the importance of hygiene, guidelines for handling raw food safely, preventing bacterial contamination, and addressing concerns related to bacterial risks.

Maintaining excellent hygiene practices when handling raw food is essential to prevent the spread of bacteria and ensure the safety of your dog and household. Here are some key points to consider:

Handwashing: Wash your hands thoroughly with soap and water before and after handling raw food. Handwashing is one of the most effective ways to prevent cross-contamination and reduce the risk of bacterial transmission.

Utensils and Surfaces: Clean and sanitize all utensils, cutting boards, and surfaces that encounter raw food. Use hot, soapy water or a dishwasher with a high-temperature sanitizing cycle to ensure proper cleanliness.

Separate Storage: Store raw food separately from other foods, especially those that are consumed raw or require minimal cooking. This separation helps minimize the risk of cross-contamination and bacterial spread.

Cleaning Practices: Regularly clean and sanitize food preparation areas, such as countertops, sinks, and storage containers. Use effective cleaning agents to eliminate any bacteria or pathogens that may be present.

When handling raw food for your dog, follow these guidelines to minimize bacterial risks:

Safe Storage: Store raw food in airtight containers or freezer bags to prevent bacterial contamination. Keep raw food stored separately from other foods, preferably in the lower portions of the refrigerator to prevent drips onto other items.

Avoid Cross-Contamination: Use separate cutting boards, knives, and utensils for raw food preparation. If possible, designate specific items solely for raw food use to avoid mixing with items used for cooked food.

Thawing Practices: Thaw raw meat and poultry in the refrigerator or use the defrost function in a microwave if immediate use is required. Avoid thawing at room temperature, as it promotes bacterial growth.

Cleaning Utensils: Wash all utensils, cutting boards, and bowls used for raw food preparation with hot, soapy water after each use. Consider using a dishwasher with a high-temperature sanitizing cycle if available.

While raw food carries a potential risk of bacterial contamination, proper handling and hygiene practices greatly minimize these risks. Here's what you can do to prevent bacterial contamination:

Trusted Sources: Source raw ingredients from reputable suppliers who follow strict quality control measures and prioritize food safety. Ensure that the meats and poultry you purchase are labeled for human consumption or meet high-quality standards.

Freshness: Choose fresh ingredients and ensure proper storage to maintain their freshness and minimize bacterial growth. Avoid using ingredients that are past their expiration dates or show signs of spoilage.

Safe Handling Temperatures: Handle raw food at safe temperatures to prevent bacterial proliferation. Keep raw ingredients refrigerated until ready for use and minimize the time they spend at room temperature during preparation.

Bacterial Risk Education: Educate yourself about the potential bacterial risks associated with raw feeding, such as Salmonella or E. coli. Understanding these risks allows you to take appropriate precautions and make informed decisions regarding your dog's diet.

Raw feeding does come with a slight risk of bacterial contamination. However, it is important to note that dogs have different digestive systems compared to humans, and they can tolerate a higher bacterial load without adverse effects. Here are some points to consider:

Natural Bacteria Tolerance: Dogs have a shorter digestive tract and a higher level of stomach acid, which helps protect them from certain bacteria. While they can still contract bacterial infections, their risk is relatively lower compared to humans.

Food Handling Precautions: Following proper hygiene practices and safe food handling techniques significantly reduces the risk of bacterial contamination. By taking appropriate precautions, you can minimize the likelihood of bacterial-related health issues.

Immunocompromised Dogs and Household Members: If your dog is immunocompromised or if there are immunocompromised individuals in your household, consult with a veterinarian or a healthcare professional for guidance on raw feeding and any additional precautions that may be necessary.

It is important to stay informed about the potential risks associated with raw feeding while implementing appropriate hygiene practices. By following proper food safety guidelines, you can minimize the risk of bacterial contamination and provide a safe raw diet for your dog.

Chapter 9: Monitoring, Exercise, and Veterinary Check-ups

Maintaining a balanced and healthy raw diet for your dog goes beyond meal preparation. In this chapter, we will explore the importance of regular monitoring, exercise, and veterinary check-ups to support your dog's overall well-being and ensure that they thrive on a raw diet.

Regular monitoring of your dog's health is essential to ensure that they are thriving on their raw diet. Here are some key areas to monitor:

Weight: Keep track of your dog's weight to ensure they are maintaining a healthy body condition. Weight fluctuations may indicate dietary imbalances or health issues that need to be addressed.

Coat and Skin: Observe the condition of your dog's coat and skin. A healthy raw diet should promote a shiny coat and clear skin free from excessive dryness, itching, or irritation.

Energy Levels: Monitor your dog's energy levels and activity. A well-balanced raw diet should provide the necessary nutrients for your dog to stay active and alert.

Digestive Health: Pay attention to your dog's digestion. Consistent gastrointestinal issues may indicate dietary sensitivities or intolerances that require adjustments to their raw diet.

Regular exercise is vital for your dog's overall well-being, regardless of the diet they are on. Engage your dog in daily physical activity, such as walks, playtime, or interactive games. Exercise not only supports their physical health but also contributes to their mental stimulation and emotional well-being.

Regular veterinary check-ups are crucial to monitor your dog's health and catch any potential issues early on. During these visits, discuss your dog's raw diet with your veterinarian, and ensure that they are receiving all the necessary nutrients for their specific life stage and health condition. Your veterinarian can also provide valuable guidance and make any necessary adjustments to their diet based on their individual needs.

Feeding your dog a raw diet can be a rewarding and healthful choice when done correctly. Prioritize proper meal preparation, food safety, and hygiene practices to minimize risks associated with raw feeding. Address common concerns and frequently asked questions to ensure you are well-informed about this dietary approach. Regularly monitor your dog's health, provide them with adequate exercise, and schedule regular veterinary check-ups to support their overall well-being and ensure they thrive on their raw diet.

Chapter 10: Conclusion and Final Thoughts

Congratulations on completing this guide to feeding your dog a raw diet! By now, you have gained a comprehensive understanding of the benefits, considerations, and practical aspects of raw feeding. As you embark on this journey with your canine companion, let's summarize the key points discussed and provide some closing thoughts.

Throughout this book, we covered a range of important topics related to feeding a raw diet to your dog. Here are the key takeaways to remember:

- Raw feeding offers numerous potential benefits, including improved digestion, dental health, coat condition, energy levels, and overall well-being for your dog.
- A raw diet should be balanced, consisting of high-quality proteins, organs, fruits, vegetables, and supplements to meet your dog's nutritional needs.
- Proper meal preparation and food safety practices are essential to prevent bacterial contamination and ensure the health of your dog and household.

- Transitioning to a raw diet should be done gradually to allow your dog's digestive system to adapt smoothly.
- Regular monitoring of your dog's health, providing exercise, and scheduling veterinary check-ups are vital for their overall well-being.

Feeding your dog a raw diet is a personal choice that requires dedication, knowledge, and a commitment to your dog's health. As you continue this journey, here are some closing thoughts to keep in mind:

- Consult with a veterinarian or a canine nutritionist: They can provide valuable guidance, address your specific concerns, and help tailor the raw diet to meet your dog's individual needs.
- Listen to your dog's needs: Each dog is unique, and their response to a raw diet may vary. Pay attention to their body condition, energy levels, and overall well-being, and adjust as necessary.
- Continue educating yourself: Stay informed about new research, developments, and best practices in raw feeding. This ongoing learning will help you provide the best possible care for your dog.
- Seek a supportive community: Connect with other raw feeding enthusiasts, join online forums or social media groups, and share experiences and knowledge. This community can offer valuable insights, support, and encouragement along your raw feeding journey.

Remember, feeding your dog a raw diet is a personal choice, and it may not be the right fit for every dog or every dog owner. It is important to make an informed decision based on your dog's individual needs, dietary requirements, and any specific health considerations.

Thank you for dedicating your time to learn about feeding your dog a raw diet. By providing a balanced and nutritious diet, you are contributing to their overall health, happiness, and longevity. Wishing you and your canine companion a wonderful journey of raw feeding and many joyful moments together!

Glossary:

1. Raw Diet: A diet that consists of uncooked and unprocessed ingredients, typically including raw meats, organs, fruits, and vegetables.

2. Nutritional Balance: The proper proportion of nutrients, vitamins, and minerals required for a balanced diet.

3. Barf Diet: An acronym for "Biologically Appropriate Raw Food" or "Bones and Raw Food," referring to a raw diet for dogs.

4. Biologically Appropriate: Foods that mimic a dog's natural diet in the wild, aiming to provide optimal nutrition.

5. Digestive Enzymes: Proteins that aid in breaking down food for better absorption and digestion.

6. Beneficial Bacteria: Microorganisms that promote a healthy gut and aid in digestion.

7. Enzymes: Biological molecules that facilitate chemical reactions in the body.

8. Macronutrients: Essential nutrients required in large quantities, such as proteins, fats, and carbohydrates.

9. Micronutrients: Essential nutrients required in smaller quantities, such as vitamins and minerals.

10. Raw Meaty Bones: Edible bones that are fed as part of a raw diet to provide dental benefits and natural calcium.

11. Prey Model: A raw feeding approach that aims to replicate a dog's natural prey diet in the wild.

12. Franken Prey Model: A modified raw feeding approach that combines various animal parts to create a balanced diet.

13. Organ Meats: Nutrient-rich meats, such as liver, kidney, heart, and spleen.

14. Meal Preparation: The process of assembling raw food ingredients to create balanced meals.

15. Food Safety: Practices to ensure that raw food is handled and prepared safely to prevent contamination.

16. Cross-Contamination: The transfer of harmful bacteria from one surface or food to another.

17. Portioning: Determining the appropriate amount of food to feed based on a dog's weight and activity level.

18. Supplements: Additional nutrients or vitamins added to a raw diet to meet specific dietary needs.

19. Dental Health: The condition of a dog's teeth and gums, which can be influenced by a raw diet.

20. Food Allergies: Adverse reactions to certain foods, which may be addressed through raw feeding.

21. Transitioning: Gradually introducing a raw diet to a dog's existing diet to avoid digestive upset.

22. Immunocompromised: A weakened immune system, which may require special considerations in raw feeding.

23. Hygiene Practices: The implementation of cleanliness measures to prevent bacterial contamination.

24. Bacterial Risks: The potential dangers associated with handling raw food, including harmful bacteria like Salmonella and E. coli.

25. Veterinarian: A qualified medical professional specializing in animal health.

26. Canine Nutritionist: An expert in formulating balanced and nutritious diets for dogs.

27. Community: A group of like-minded individuals who share
    knowledge and experiences related to raw feeding.

28. Body Condition: The physical state of a dog's body, including
    weight and muscle mass.

29. Veterinary Check-ups: Regular visits to a veterinarian to monitor a
    dog's health and address any concerns.

www.ingramcontent.com/pod-product-compliance
Lightning Source LLC
Chambersburg PA
CBHW070225260726
48658CB00006BA/2175